THE
VINTAGE
DOG DIARY

- THE DACHSHUND -

British Library Cataloguing-in-Publication Data
A catalogue record for this book is available from
the British Library

VDB

www.vintagedogbooks.com

THE DACHSHUND EARL SATIN BY EARL BULLER—COUNTESS TEKLA

THE PROPERTY OF MISS M. W. V. HAWKINS, HAYFORD HALL, BUCKFASTLEIGH

FROM THE PAINTING BY LILIAN CHEVIOT

Lilian Cheviot 1908.

MR. CLAUDE WOODHEAD'S
CH. BRANDESBURTON MIMOSA
BY CH. SLOAN——TOSCA.

JANUARY

For love, that comes wherever life and sense
Are given by God, in thee was most intense;
A chain of heart, a feeling of the mind,
A tender sympathy, which did thee bind
Not only to us men, but to thy kind;
Yea, for thy fellow brutes in thee we saw
A soul of love, love's intellectual law;
Hence, if we wept, it was not done in shame,
Our tears from passion and from reason came;
And therefore shalt thou be an honoured name

WORDSWORTH. Tribute to a Dog

MY lord Archbishop, may I come in with my dog?
TENNYSON. *Becket*, Act i., scene iv.

IF I can be as good a brute as my dog here...
    I shall be very well content.
KINGSLEY. *Hypatia*

POOR dog! He was faithful and kind to be sure,
And constantly loved me; although I was poor.
CAMPBELL. *Poor Dog Tray.*

ASK my dog: if he say "aye," it wilt;
If he say "no," it wilt.
If he say nothing, and shake his tail, it will.
SHAKESPEARE. *Two Gentlemen of Verona, ii. 5.*

WHAT the devil do you come between me and my dog
for?
DICKENS. *Oliver Twist.*

CALLS to the few tired dogs that yet remain:
Blanch, Swift, and Music, noblest of their kind.
WORDSWORTH. *Hart-Leap Well.*

GOOD dog Tray is happy now;
He has no time to say "Bow-wow!"
STRUWELPETER. *Naughty Frederick.*

MY dog shall mortify the pride of man's superior breed.
COWPER. *The Dog and the Water-Lily.*

MRS. A. L. DEWAR'S RED BITCH

CH. LENCHEN

BY CH. SNAKES PRINCE——FASHODA.

BUT if I be I, as I suppose I be;
Then I've a little dog at home, and he knows me.
Old Ballad.

SIR, he is a good dog, and a fair dog;
Can there be more said; he is good and fair.
SHAKESPEARE. *Merry Wives of Windsor, i. I*

"TWO heads are better than one," quoth the
woman when she took her dog to market
with her.
Old Proverb.

A SLAUGHTERMAN'S tulip-eared puppy is as
liable to engage one's liking as his chuckle-
headed master.
T. HOOD.

MY spaniel, prettiest of his race,
And high in pedigree
COWPER. *The Dog and the Water-Lily*

A TRAVELLER, by the faithful hound,
Half-buried in the snow, was found.
LONGFELLOW. *Excelsior*

AND God lives in you too – and all your kind.
Yes, good dog, you king of beasts, I see it in
your eyes.
DU MAURIER. *Trilby.*

… I HAVE dogs, my lord,
Will rouse the proudest panther in the chase
And climb the highest promontory rock.
SHAKESPEARE. *Titus Andronicus, ii. 2.*

YOU must thank my teacher, the dog – not
me.
KINGSLEY. *Hypatia.*

THERE was speech in their dumbness,
language in their very gesture.
SHAKESPEARE. *Winter's Tale, v. 3.*

THE hindmost dog may catch the hare.
Old Proverb.

THE sport may be lost by a moment's delay,
So whip up the puppies and scurry away.
KINGSLEY. *The Find.*

MISS M. W. S. HAWKINS' LONG-HAIRED
DACHSHUND ALEXANDER SCHNAPPS
BY SCHNAPPS——ALEX.

THY wit is as quick as the greyhound's
mouth – it catches.
SHAKESPEARE. *Much Ado about Nothing, v. 2*

HE'D make a fortin; on the stage, that dog
would, and rewive the drama.
DICKENS. *Oliver Twist.*

ALWAYS give your dog, like your wife, their
own way. It saves trouble, as they are
sure to get it in the end.
R. J. LLOYD PRICE. *Dog's Tales.*

UNG roy, ung loy, ung chien.
Old Motto.

Oh spare the dog – it saved my father.
KINGSLEY. *Hypatia.*

JANUARY 25

I AM his Highness' dog at Kew;
Pray tell me, sir, whose dog are you?
POPE. *A collar inscription.*

JANUARY 26

A LIVING dog is better than a dead lion.
Eccl. ix. 4.

JANUARY 27

DIDST thou think that I should be faithless
and forsake thee – I, a dog?
OUIDA. *Dog of Flanders.*

JANUARY 28

I THINK the tenderness, chivalry, fidelity, and
prudence of that dog would make a fair
share of virtue for any human being.
R. J. LLOYD PRICE. *Dog's Tales*

THOU callest me "a dog" without a cause;
But since I am a dog – beware my fangs.
SHAKESPEARE. *Merchant of Venice, iii. 3.*

FOUR dogs, each different breed;
Distinguished, two for scent, and two speed.
WORDSWORTH. *A Dog's Tragedy.*

I HAVE all my life had a sympathy for mongrel,
ungainly dogs, who are nobody's pets.
GEORGE ELIOT. *Scenes from Clerical Life.*

'Tis a good dog can catch anything.
Proverb.

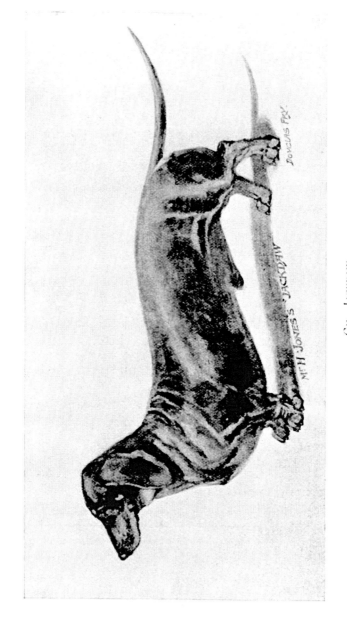

MR H. JONES'S "JACKDAW"   BOWDEN FECIT.

CH. JACKDAW.

FEBRUARY

But the poor dog, in life the firmest friend,
The first to welcome, foremost to defend.
Whose honest heart is still his master's own,
Who labours, fights, lives, breathes for him alone,
Unhonoured falls; unnoticed all his worth,
Denied in heaven, the love he held on earth.
While man, vile insect, hopes to be forgiven,
And claims himself a sole, exclusive Heaven.

BYRON. To a Dog.

BETTER thy dog than thee. . . . Poor beast!
Poor beast! Set him down. I will bind
up his wounds with my napkin. Give
him a bone.
TENNYSON. *Becket.*

BEHIND them followed the watch-dog,
Patient, full of importance, and grand in the
pride of his instinct,
Walking from side to side with a lordly air,
and superbly waving his bushy tail.
LONGFELLOW. *Evangeline.*

BUT of *thee* it shall be said,
This dog watched beside a bed,
Day and night unweary. . . .
E. B. BROWNING. *To my Dog.*

HE payeth best who loveth best
All things both great and small.
COLERIDGE. *Ancient Mariner*

HUNTSMAN, I charge thee, tender well my
hounds. . . .
Tomorrow I intend to hunt again.
SHAKESPEARE. *Taming of the Shrew, i.*

AND as for dogges; Dr. Caynes, a learned
Phisition and a good man, wrote a treatise
of them, and Scriptur itself hath vouch-
safed to commend Tobias Dogge.
HARINGTON. 1591

A SMALL old Spaniel, which had been Don José's
His father, whom he loved as ye may think,
For on such things the memory reposes
With tenderness.
BYRON. *Don Juan*

THE old man shall not be deprived of his
faithful dog. I would I had any creature,
were it only a dog, that followed me
because it loved me, not for what it could
make of me.
SCOTT. *Woodstock.*

CH. JACKDAW
when 13 years old.

HE was a gash an' faithfu' tyke
As ever lap a sheugh or dyke;
His honest, sonsie, bawsn't face,
Aye gat him friends in ika place.
BURNS. *The Twa Dogs.*

WITH two brave sheep-dogs tried in many a
storm,
The one of an inestimable worth,
Made all their household.
WORDWORTH. *Michael.*

AND I am recompensed, and deem the toils
Of poetry not lost, if verse of mine
May stand between an animal and woe
And teach one tyrant pity for his drudge.
COWPER. *The Task, Book vi.*

. . . THE wise old hound,
Regardless of the frolic pack, attends
His master's side, or slumbers at his ease
Beneath the bending shade.
SOMERVILLE.

I WOULD not lose the dog for twenty pounds.
SHAKESPEARE. *Taming of the Shrew, Act i.*

QUIET, Vixen! You're like the rest of the women
– always putting in your word before you
know why.
GEORGE ELLIOT. *Adam Bede*

POOR beastie; he's some value, surely, I' God's
sight.
OUIDA. *Puck.*

IS it not enough to have nine blind puppies at
my back, and an old brute at my heels who
will persist in saving my life.
KINGSLEY. *Hypatia.*

LIKE angry dogs that snarl at first, and then
display their teeth.
T. HOOD. *The Sea-Spell.*

CHIEN qui abbaye, ne mord pas.
Old Proverb.

MY heart is great; but it must break with
silence.
SHAKESPEARE. *Richard II., ii. I.*

AY, ay, let the dog have the best.
OUIDA. *Dog of Flanders.*

A HUGE nondescript sort of a dog, built up of
every breed in France, with the virtues of
all and the vices of none.
DU MAURIER. *Trilby.*

FOR my part I do wish thou wert a dog
That I might love thee.
SHAKESPEARE. *Timon of Athens, iv. 3.*

CH. WIRRAL HOLLYBRANCH.

A Pet – a favourite pug – whose squat figure,
black muzzle, and tortuosity of tail that
curled like a head of celery in a salad bowl,
bespoke his Dutch extraction.
Ingoldsby Legends. *Spectre of Tappington.*

WHEN Peggy's dog her arms imprison,
I often wish my lot was hisn.
T. HOOD. *Huggins and Duggins.*

I COULDN'T have any other dog but Jip – it
would be so unkind. Besides I couldn't
be such friends with any other dog but
Jip, because he wouldn't have known me
before I was married.
DICKENS. *David Copperfield.*

I ONCE had a hound, a right good hound,
    A hound both fleet and strong;
He ate my board, and slept by my bed,
    And ran with me, all day long.
KINGSLEY. *Saint's Tragedy.*

AS true a dog as ever fought at head.
SHAKESPEARE. *Titus Andronicus,*
Act v. scene i.

CANE vaccio non baia indarno.
Italian Proverb.

No sycophant, although of Spaniel race,
And though no hound, a martyr to the chase.
COWPER. *Epitaph on Top, the Dog.*

ALONE with that his faithful dog,
Then old, beside him lying at his feet.
WORDSWORTH. *Michael.*

HIS breast was white, his towzie back
Weel clad wi' coat of glossy black;
His gawnie tail, wi' upward curl,
Hung o'er his hurdies wi' a swirl.
BURNS. *The Twa Dogs.*

TIME, stern huntsman, who can balk,
Staunch as hound, and fleet as hawk.
SCOTT. *Hunting Song.*

THE DACHSHUND

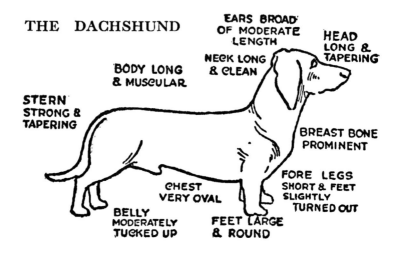

EARS BROAD OF MODERATE LENGTH

HEAD LONG & TAPERING

NECK LONG & CLEAN

BODY LONG & MUSCULAR

STERN STRONG & TAPERING

BREAST BONE PROMINENT

FORE LEGS SHORT & FEET SLIGHTLY TURNED OUT

CHEST VERY OVAL

BELLY MODERATELY TUCKED UP

FEET LARGE & ROUND

MARCH

*Aye, sir, that's a pity, begging your pardon
. . . it's a great pity that; beast or body,
education should aye be minded. I have
six terriers at hame, forbye twa couple
of slow hunas, five grews, and a wheen
other dogs. There's auld Pepper and auld
Mustard, and young Pepper and young
Mustard, and little Pepper and little
Mustard. I had them a' regularly entered,
first in rottens, then wi' stots or weasels,
and then wi' the tods and brocks, and now
they fear naething that ever cam wi' a
hairy skin on't.*

SCOTT. Guy Mannering.

... I REMEMBERED then
Thy faithful fondness; for not mean the joy
I felt from they dumb welcome.
SOUTHEY. *On the Death of a Favourite Spaniel.*

IN truth he was a peerless hound.
SPENSER. *Gelert.*

QUI aime Jean, aime son Chien.
French Proverb.

IT was a litter – a litter of five,
Four were drowned, and one left alive.
He was thought worthy alone to survive.
Ingoldsby Legends. Bagman's Dog.

GIVE to dogs what though wouldst deny to men.
SHAKESPEARE. *Timon of Athens, iv. 3.*

LITTLE dogs start the hare, but great ones
catch it.
Old Proverb.

HE was not a big dog when I bought him, but
just a little ball of orange-tawny fluff that I
  could carry with one hand. His power
of affection increased with his weight.
DU MAURIER. *Trilby.*

BELIEVE me, friend Latimer, I would as soon
expose my faithful household dog to a
vain combat with a herd of wolves.
SCOTT. *Redgauntlet.*

SHAGGY, and lean, and shrewd, with pointed ears,
And tail cropped short; half lurcher and half cur.
His dog attends him!
COWPER. *The Task, Book v.*

THE tither was a ploughman's collie,
A rhyming, ranting, raving billie.
BURNS. *The Twa Dogs.*

[Photo] [E.N.A.

A LONG-HAIRED DACHSHUND.

In their native Germany Dachshunds are used as their name implies to hunt badgers, their curiously shaped front feet being specially adapted for digging. The dog shown in the picture is seen with its owner, Fräulein Friedl Czepa, of Vienna, who is said to have paid £250 for it to a London dealer.

POOR dog, he was faithful and kind to be sure,
He constantly loved me, although I was poor;
When sour-looking folk sent me heartless away,
I had always a friend in my poor dog Tray.
CAMPBELL.

THE little dogs and all,
Tray, Blanche, and Sweetheart – see, they bark
at me.
SHAKESPEARE. *King Lear, Act. iii. Scene vi.*

A BONNY terrier that, sir, and a fell chield at
the vermin, I warrant him – that is, if he's
been well entered, for it a' lies i' that.
SCOTT. *Guy Mannering.*

A TERRIER, too, that once had been a Briton's,
Who, dying on the coast of Ithica,
The peasants gave the poor dumb thing a pittance.
BYRON. *Don Juan.*

DOGS think a great deal; when people believe
us asleep nine times out of ten we are
meditating.
OUIDA. *Puck.*

THE wakeful bloodhound rose, and shook his
hide,
But his sagacious eye an inmate owns.
KEATS. *Eve of S. Agnes.*

THIS dog only, waited on,
Knowing that when light is gone,
Love remains for shining.
E. B. BROWNING. *To Flush, my Dog.*

REGENT of flocks was he when the shepherd
slept; their protector
When from the forest at night, through the
starry silence, the wolves howled.
LONGFELLOW. *Evangeline.*

WHO misuses a dog would misuse a child . . .
they cannot speak for themselves. . . . God
help him!
TENNYSON. *Becket.*

AND . . . well, the dog was game.
BRET HARTE. *The Hawk's Nest.*

FOREMOST . . . whatever dog was there!
MARY RUSSELL MITFORD.

EACH dog barks in his own yard.
R. KIPLING. *Jungle Book.*

SAE that the hound him lovit sae
That he will part nae wise him frae.
BARBOUR. *Bruce and the Bloodhound.*

AND with a courtly grin the fawning hound
Salutes thee cowering.
SOMERVILLE. *The Chase.*

Photo]   *[Sport and General*

A NOTED GERMAN BREED.

There are three types of Dachshund—the smooth, the wire-coated, and the long-haired, all of which are extremely intelligent and make excellent companions. Here are three smooth-coated members of a famous kennel "Kailora" "Karzaire", and "Karzador", the property of Miss F. E. Dixon.

DOGS gnaw their bones because they cannot
swallow them.
Italian Proverb.

A TAME cheater, i' faith;
You may stroke him as gently as a puppy
greyhound.
SHAKESPEARE. *Henry IV., ii. 4.*

YOUR faithful soldiers . . . follow you like
dogs, fight for you like dogs, and have
the grave of a dog on the spot where they
happen to fall.
SCOTT. *Woodstock.*

A GOOD dog deserves a good home.
Old Proverb.

HOW in his mid-career, the setter, struck
Stiff, by the tainted gale, with open nose
Outstretched, and finely sensible . . .
THOMPSON.

TWO wifies in one house,
Two catties and one mouse,
Two doggies and one bone,
Never did agree in one.
UNKNOWN.

EVEN a wise man may become attached to
a dog.
GOETHE.

THE dog who barks loudest is not always the
best watcher.
DOWNEY.

THEY watch to hear the bloodhound baying,
They watch to hear the war-horn braying.
SCOTT, *Lay of the Last Minstrel.*

A DOG in office, set to bark
All beggars from his door!
T. HOOD. *Ode to H. Bodkin.*

LITTLE Flo, a tiny spaniel of the Blenheim
breed, bounced out from beneath a sofa
and began to bark at . . . his pantaloons!
Ingoldsby Legends. Spectre of Tappington.

Photo]   *[Sport & General.*

THE LONG-HAIRED VARIETY OF THE GERMAN BADGER DOG.

Long-haired Dachshunds have been known in Germany for well over a hundred years, but are still not as popular as the short-coated variety. Two distinguished dogs are shown in the picture, Miss K. E. Allinson's "Kalje of Bromholm" and "Gamester of Bromholm".

APRIL

Near this spot
Are deposited the remains of one
Who possessed Beauty without Vanity,
Strength without Insolence,
Courage without Ferocity,
And all the Virtues of Man without
his Vices.
This Praise, which would be unmeaning
Flattery
If inscribed over human ashes,
Is but a just tribute to the Memory
of a Dog.

BYRON. Epitaph.

REMEMBEREST thou my greyhound true?
O'er holt and hill there never flew,
From slip or leash there never sprang
More fleet of foot, or sure of fang.
SCOTT. *Marmion.*

BY all beloved and loving all,
My Marmion! Favourite of the hall!
MARY RUSSELL MITFORD.

QUAND un chien se noye, chacun lui offer a
boire.
French Proverb.

NOW let your nose be as keen as beagles,
Your steps as swift as greyhounds.
SHELLEY. *Oedipus Tyrannus.*

THE dog had watched about the spot, or by his
master's side.
How nourished here, through such long time,
He knows, who gave that love sublime.
WORDSWORTH. *Fidelity.*

THE watch-dog's voice, that bayed the whispering
wind!
GOLDSMITH.

HE listens for his trusty hounds.
SCOTT. *The Wild Huntsman.*

A MASTIFF of true English blood
Loved fighting better than his food.
When dogs are snarling for a bone
He longed to make the war his own,
And often found (where two contend)
To interpose obtained his end.
GAY. *Meddling Mastiff.*

Photo]   [*Hugh D. Martineau.*

GOOD COMPANIONS.

The Dachshund is good company, gentle and faithful, as well
as being one of the best "guards" among the smaller dogs.

THE dog is not of mountain breed;
Its motions, too, are wild and shy.
WORDWORTH. *Fidelity.*

OH! . . . to be like you, good dog . . . and
secrete love and goodwill, from morn till
night – from night till morn.
DU MAURIER. *Trilby.*

WE are apt to be kinder to the brutes that
love us than to the women that love
us. Is it because the brutes are dumb?
GEORGE ELIOT. *Adam Bede.*

A LOVING creature she, and brave,
And fondly tries her struggling friend to save.
WORDSWORTH. *A Dog's Tragedy.*

HIS good hound for weal or woe,
Would not from his master go,
Buy lay licking his woundes.
He meanys to have helped him again,
Thereto he did all his main;
Great kindness is in houndis.
Mediaeval Metrical Romance.

NOT for myself. . . . I assure you. Like Atè's
golden apple, it shall go to the fairest.
. . . Here, Bran!
KINGSLEY. *Hypatia.*

WELL of all dogs it stands confessed
Your English bulldogs are the best.
I say it, and will set my hand to 't,
Camden records it, and I'll stand to 't.
SMART. *Insular Prejudice.*

NATURE never makes a ferret in the shape of
a mastiff.
GEORGE ELIOT.

MUST I feel an equal warmth towards my
bosom friend and his greyhound?
T. HOOD.

THE fleetest, bravest hound
That ever coursed on hill or lea,
Or swept the heathy ground.
MARY RUSSELL MITFORD.

A FRANKLYN'S dogge leped over a style,
And hys name was littel Byngo.
Ingoldsby Legends. Lay of S. Glenulphus.

SO, when two dogs are fighting in the streets,
With a third dog, one of the two dogs meets,
With angry teeth he beats him to the bone,
And this dog smarts for what that dog has done.
FIELDING. *Tom Thumb the Great.*

[Post Foppen.

THE SMOOTH DACHSHUND.

The breed has gradually become more and more popular in Britain. The above are typical specimens, showing their remarkable ears and shortness of leg.

[Photo.

WELL, dogs cannot lie, or bribe, or pick a lock,
Or go bull-baiting in share markets, or pre-side
As chairmen over public companies!
OUIDA. *Puck.*

HERE lies poor Nick, an honest creature,
Of faithful, gently, courteous nature.
SYDNEY SMITH.

CALM, though not mean, courageous without rage,
Serious not dull, and without thinking, sage:
Pleased at the lot that nature has assigned,
Snarl as I list, and freely bark my mind.
W. HAMILTON. *The Dog Incog.*

HE has known me in all that has happened;
haven't you, Jip? And I couldn't bear to
slight him because he was a little altered.
DICKENS. *David Copperfield.*

I DO allow him to be as familiar with me as
my dog.
SHAKESPEARE. *Henry IV., ii. 2.*

I ROSE with the dawn: with my dog as my
guide.
BYRON. *Young Highlander.*

BUT Maddalo was travelling far away,
Among the mountains of Armenia.
His dog was dead.
SHELLEY. *Julian and Maddalo.*

OTHER dogs in thymey dew
Tracked the hares and followed through
Sunny moor and meadow. . . .
E. B. BROWNING. *To my Dog.*

ALL the hedges are white with dust, and the
great dog under the creaking wain
Hangs his head in the lazy heat, while onward
the horses toil and strain.
LONGFELLOW. *The Golden Legend.*

GIVE a child while he craves, and a dog while
his tail doth wag, and you shall have a
fair dog and a foul knave.
Old Proverb.

NOTES

[Photo] "MR. WEBSTER" AND THE COUNTESS. [Hay Wrightson.
A great lover of animals, the Countess of Northesk is here seen with her favourite Dachshund, "Mr. Webster".

MAY

A sensible dog takes human beings as he finds them. They have their good points and their bad points (some have no points at all), but they mean well, and they are the most intelligent animals we have.

STEPHEN TOWNSEND.
A Thoroughbred Mongrel.

AND close beside him, in the snow,
Poor Yarrow, partner of their woe,
Crouches upon his master's breast
And licks his cheek to break his rest.
SCOTT. *Marmion.*

AS true a dog as ever fought at head.
SHAKESPEARE. *King Lear, iv. 6.*

He'd been a good 'un in his time.
HORSFIELD.

I OFFERED her my own, who is a dog as big
as ten of yours, and therefore a gift the
greater.
SHAKESPEARE. *Two Gentlemen of Verona, iv. 4.*

WE canna meet Him no fairer, no better, than
wi' hands as niver hae harmed the poor
dumb beast.
OUIDA. *Puck.*

HE was a joy. It was good to go to sleep
and know he would be there in the
morning.
DU MAURIER. *Trilby.*

THE deep-mouthed bark
Comes nigher still and nigher;
Bursts on the path a dark bloodhound,
His tawny muzzle tracked the ground,
And his red eye shot fire.
SCOTT. *Lay of the Last Minstrel.*

OH! Where does faithful Gelert roam,
The flower of his race?
So true, so brave; a lamb at home,
A lion in the chase!
SPENSER. *Gelert*

A LOVING creature, she, and brave.
WORDSWORTH. *Incident.*

DOGS bark as they are bred. . . .
Old Proverb.

A CHARMING PICTURE.

Viscountess Harcourt, with her two babies, and a Smooth-haired Dachshund, their constant companion.
Dachshunds make admirable pets for children, because they are so even-tempered, kind, and reliable.

QUIEN a su péno quiere matar,
Eabia le ha levantar.
Spanish Proverb.

NO serious order did he e'er forget,
    No loving friend;
He was as true a heart as could be met
    To the world's end.
HORNE. *Beth Gellert.*

AND yet thou should'st have lived!
SOUTHEY. *On the Death of a Favourite Dog.*

LOVE me, love my dog. . . .
Proverb.

WHEN I feel happy my tail almost wags me
off my legs, but when I pretend to be
happy, it flops about with as much spirit
as a wet rag on a still day.
STEPHEN TOWNSEND.

FIERCE, bounding sprang the ship,
Like greyhound starting from the slip
To seize his flying prey.
SCOTT. *Lord of the Isles.*

AND in that town a dog was found,
As many dogs there be;
Both mongrel, puppy, whelp, and hound,
And curs of low degree.
GOLDSMITH. *Mad Dog.*

IF Gyp had had a tail he would doubtless have
wagged it, but being destitute of that
vehicle for his emotions, he was, like many
other worthy persons, destined to appear
more phlegmatic than nature had made him.
GEORGE ELIOT. *Adam Bede.*

THIS dog only . . . crept and crept
Next a languid cheek that slept,
Sharing in the shadow.
E. B. BROWNING. *To Flush.*

MEN who loved dogs were always pitiful.
OUIDA.

I SHALL make Jip race, he is getting quite
old and lazy.
DICKENS. *David Copperfield.*

SHE could turn a knight into a wagon of hay,
Or two nice little boys into puppies at play.
Ingoldsby Legends. Bleeding Heart Yard.

AS a dog keeps his master's root,
Bidding the plunderer stand aloof.
SCOTT. *Rokeby.*

HE wasn't a bit intellectual, and thought more
of chasing a sheep on the hillside than of
psychological discussion.
TOWNSEND. *A Thoroughbred Mongrel.*

Photo] [*B.I.P.*

KEEPING OUT OF THE COLD.

In April 1934 a Dachshund Show was held at Tattersall's. Our picture shows Mrs. D. W. Elliott, the well-known breeder, keeping her three entries warmly covered with a rug.

THE deep-mouthed bloodhound's heavy bay
Resounded up the rocky way.
SCOTT. *Lady of the Lake.*

TWO curs shall tame each other: pride alone
Must tarre the mastiffs on, as 'twere their bone.
SHAKESPEARE. *Troilus and Cressida, i. 3.*

A PARLOUR pet unspoiled by favour,
A pattern of good dog behaviour.
SYDNEY SMITH.

MY love shall hear the music of my hounds
Uncouple in the western valley; let them go.
SHAKESPEARE. *Midsummer Night's Dream, iv. I.*

HE that strikes my dog would strike me, if he
durst.
Old Proverb.

LOOK! A horse at the door,
      And little King Charley snarling!
Go back, my lord, across the moor,
      You are not her darling.
TENNYSON. *Maud, xii. 8.*

IN a corner of the buzzing shade
The house-dog, with the vacant greyhound, lies
Outstretched and sleepy.
THOMSON. *Seasons.*

NATURE teaches beasts to know their friends.
SHAKESPEARE. *Coriolanus, ii. I.*

DOGS that bark at a distance never bite.
Old Proverb.

IF you will couple up an ordinary low-country
greyhound with a Highland wolf-dog, you
must not blame the first of them for
taking the direction it pleases the last to
drag him in.
SCOTT. *Fair Maid of Perth.*

TWO dogs strive for a bone and the third runs
away with it.
Proverb.

THEY called us – for our fierceness – English
dogs!
SHAKESPEARE. *Henry VI., i. 5.*

GIVE a dog a bad name and you may as well
hang him.
Proverb.

FROM STYRIA.

Styria is the Dachshund's native land. Here is a Styrian lad, in national costume
with his Smooth and Long-haired "Dackrels".

JUNE

They were friends in a friendship closer than brotherhood. . . . His heart awakened to a mighty love, which never wavered once in its fidelity while life abode with him. . . . And being a dog he was grateful.

OUIDA. Dog of Flanders.

WHEN mastiffs fight, little dogs bark.
Old Proverb.

THE fleetest hound in all the North.
SCOTT. *Lady of the Lake.*

TO assume a semblance the very dogs dis-
claimed.
SHAKESPEARE. *King Lear, iv. 6.*

ON the drawbridge the warder stout,
Saw a terrier and lurcher passing out.
SCOTT. *Lay of the Last Minstrel.*

THE shepherd doth not kill the sheep that
wander from his flock, but send
His careful dog to bring them to the fold.
TENNYSON. *Queen Mary, iii. 4.*

SOUVENT à mauvais chien tombe un bon os
en gueule.
French Proverb.

WHEN every terrier rough and grim,
And greyhound with his length of limb;
And pointer, now employ'd no more,
Cumber our parlour's narrow floor.
SCOTT. *Marmion.*

IF the dog bark, go in;
If the bitch bark, go out.
Hebrew Proberb.

THE first I'll name, they ca'd him Caesar,
Was keepit for his Honour's pleasure;
His hair, his size, his mouth, his lugs,
Show'd he was nane o' Scotland's dogs.
BURNS. *The Twa Dogs.*

[Photo]

A CANINE HELPER.

[L.N.A.

"Astra", a Miniature Long-haired Dachshund, entered for Tattersall's Dachshund Dog Show, is assisting a juvenile programme seller.

BETTER to be a liar's dog, and hold my master
honest.
TENNYSON. *Harold III., I.*

HIS good hound, for weal or woe,
Would not from his master go.
UNKNOWN. *Mediaeval Romance.*

MY spaniel, prettiest of his race,
And high in pedigree.
COWPER. *Dog and Water-Lily.*

SIR WALTER, restless as the veering wind,
Calls to the few tired dogs that yet remain.
WORDSWORTH. *Hart-Leap Well.*

FORESTERS in green-wood trim
Lead in the leash the gazehounds grim
SCOTT. *Marmion.*

THEN from the plaintive mother's teat he took
Her blind and shuddering puppies, naming each,
And naming those, his friends, for whom they were.
TENNYSON. *The Brook.*

THE best dog leaps the stile first.

DOGS that put up many hares, eat none.
Old Proverbs.

THOU didst love to lick the hand that fed thee;
Even life itself was comfort.
SOUTHEY. *On the Death of a Dog.*

Greg's Birthday – give big present (!!)
take to dinner

HE looked the oddest, wee-set, waywardest,
most whimsical little doglet in the world.
TOWNSEND. *Thoroughbred Mongrel.*

THERE was Yap, the queer white and brown
terrier, with one ear turned back, trotting
about and sniffing vaguely, as though he
were in search of a companion.
GEORGE ELIOT. *Mill on the Floss.*

GET thee hence and find my dog again.
SHAKESPEARE. *Two Gentlemen of Verona, iv. 4.*

HE could carry, and fetch, and run after a stick,
Could well understand, the word of command.
Ingoldsby Legends. Bagman's Dog.

Photo]   [*E.N.A.*

A BEVY OF BEAUTIES.

Fräulein Maria Paudler, particularly well known as the star of the German Talkie version of "Waltzes from Vienna", is a great dog-lover. The dog on the left is a Long-haired Dachshund.

"WE hounds killed the hare," quoth the lapdog.
Old Proverb.

LET a be the hound, man, let a be the hound;
Kilbuck mauna be guided that gate
neither.
SCOTT. *Black Dwarf.*

CAÓ que muito ladra nunca bom pera caça.
Portuguese Proverb.

I CARRIED Mistress Silvia the dog you bade me.
SHAKESPEARE. *Two Gentlemen of Verona, iv. 4.*

EVERY dog is eager hearted.
WORDSWORTH. *Incident.*

MY dog, now lost in flags and reeds,
    Now starting into sight;
Pursued the swallow on the mead
    With scarce a slower flight.
COWPER. *Beau and the Water-Lily.*

FORTUNATELY we dogs have powers of tele-
pathy unknown to humans.
TOWNSEND. *Thoroughbred Mongrel.*

HIS valour and his vigilance
Became a proverb of the vale;
His instincts made a small romance,
And shepherd boys preserved each tale.
HORNE.

THE slowhound wakes the fox's lair,
The greyhound presses on the hare.
SCOTT. *Rokeby.*

HE'S gone to seek his dog; which, by his
master's commands, he must carry for a
present to his lady.
SHAKESPEARE. *Two Gentlemen of Verona, iv. 2.*

NOTES

Photo]   [*Sport and General.*

IN THE HANDS OF THE JUDGE.

The picture of the Countess Reventlow (of Denmark) judging Wire-haired Dachshunds at a Kennel Club Show. Notice the dappled colouring of the dog furthest from the camera.

JULY

It is easy enough to cock one's ears and to caper about with a fictitious gaiety, but the tail has a personality of its own, and always gives us dogs away....if only I had my tail under control, I should be the most successful and charming liar in the world.

TOWNSEND.
A Thoroughbred Mongrel.

THE almighty, who gave the dog to be the
companion of our pleasures and out toils,
hath invested him with a nature noble
and incapable of deceit.
SIR WALTER SCOTT.

SO they went fourth both, and the young man's
dog with them.
Tobit, v. 16

WITH eye upraised, his master's look to scan,
The joy, the solace, and the aid of man.
CRABBE.

HE followit him where'er he gaed,
Sae that the hound him lovit sae,
That he wald part nae wise him frae.
BARBOUR. *Bruce and the blood hound*

A dog howls loud and long,
And now, as guided by the voice of Heaven,
Digs with his feet, …
A man lies underneath! Let us to work.
ROGERS. *Barry the St. Bernard.*

…EVEN to the beast
That lacks discourse of reason, but too oft
With uncorrupted feeling and dumb faith
Puts lordly man to shame.
SOUTHEY. *Roderick's Faithful Theron.*

SO all forsook him, all save one –
One humble, faithful, powerless slave-
His dog, old Nina.
CAROLINE SOUTHEY. *The Tale of Reign of Terrier.*

NEVER was a puppy so *bien instruit,*
Or possessed of such natural talent, as he.
BARHAM. *Bagman's Dog.*

A CHARMING LOT.

Miss Pamela Howard, with her mother's extremely attractive Miniature Dachshunds, at the Club's Jubilee Show at Tattersall's, London, in 1935.

THE rich man's guardian, and the poor man's
friend;
The only creature faithful to the end.
CRABBE.

THOUGH the mastiff be gentle, yet bite him
not on the lip.
Old proverb

HIS faithful dog, rough Gelert, wit them sped,
…He was as true as heart as could be met
To the world's end.
HORNE. *Beth Gelert.*

ALL human ties alas! Are ropes of sand,
… But never yet the dog our bounty fed,
Betrayed the kindness, or forgot the bread.
LYTTON. *Gwaine and the Hound.*

BY the angel Raphael guided,
Went the faithful dog, and good.
MARY HOWITT. *Tobias' Dog*

FAÄITHFUL an' True- them words be i' Scriptur
-an' Faäithful an' True
'Ull be fun' upo' four short legs ten times fur
one an' upo' two.
TENNYSON. *Owd Roä*

SIGN me a hero!...
Over the balustrade has bounced
A mere, instinctive dog...
How well he dives!
R.BONING. *Tray: A Hero*

THE knight had another jewel
That he loved so well:
A greyhound that was good and snel,
And the knight loved it well.
UNKNOWN. *Medieval Romance.*

OH, Indra, and what of this dog? It hath
faithfully followed me through:
Let it go with me into heaven, for my soul
is full of compassion.
Indian Hero's Creed.

MY hounds are bred out of the Spartan kind,
So flewed, so sanded;...
Matched in mouth like bells-
A cry more tuneable was never hollaed to.
SHAKESPEARE . *Sonnet*

NOR last, forget my faithful dogs.
DRYDEN
'TIS an ill dog that deserves not a crust.
Old proverb.

I WAS a dog much in respect for doughty deed.
HAMILTON. *Bonny Heck.*

THE DACHSHUND   Ruben von de Jowitt

A ROLICKSOME, frolicsome, rare old cock
As ever did nothing was our dog Jock;
A gleesome, fleasome, affectionate beast,
As slow at a fight, as swift at a feast.
PAYN. *Our Dog Jock.*

YOU are not so old,Jiip, are you, that you'll
leave your mother yet? We may keep
each other a little longer.
DICKENS. *David Copperfield.*

TRUSTED and faithful, tried and true,
Watchful and swift to do my will;
Grateful for care that was thy due,
To duty's call obedient still.
FANNY KEMBLE. *On an Irish Terrier.*

KIND and courteous, and faithful and true,
Qualities, Tray, that were found in you.
BARHAM. *The Cynotaph.*

PRAY steal me not; I'm Mrs. Dingley's,
Whose heart in this four footed thing lies.
SWIFT. *On The Collar of a Tiger.*

MY Bawty is a cur I dearly like.
RAMSEY

BRAG is a good dog but Holdfast is better.
Old Proverb.

MY dog, the trustiest of his kind,
With gratitude inflames my mind;
I mark his true, his faithful way,
And in my service copy Tray.
GAY. *Tray, the Exemplar.*

MY master wants no key of state,
For Bounce can keep his house and gate.
UNKNOWN

I HAVE known many so-called Christians who
have neither the amiability nor the dis-
crimination of this dog.
GEORGE LEWES.

TRUELOVE, his hound so good,
Helped his master, and by him stood.
Mediaval Romance.

WHEN fatigued, on the grass the shepherd
would lie...
His faithful companion crawled constantly
nigh.
PETER PINDAR. *Old Friends.*

THE DACHSHUND   TANTIVEY MATILDA

AUGUST

Dogs are judges of character, and are seldom mistaken in their intuitive likes and dislikes. There is no animal possessing one tithe of the qualifications of the dog for the various purposes by which he is used by man — a woman's pet, a man's companion, a vigilant sentry, a powerful and valiant ally, and the most faithful and truest of friends.

HENTY.

THIS dog only, watched in reach
Of a faintly-uttered speech
Or a louder sighing.
E.B. Browning. *To Flush*.

AND now I'm in the world alone-
But why should I for others groan
When none will sigh for me?
Perhaps my dog will whine in vain.
BYRON. *Childe Harold*.

HE has the staunch Cyme-hound to track the
wounded buck hill and dale; but he
hath also the fleet gazehound to kill him
at view.
SIR W SCOTT. *Kenilworth*.

THEY were coming, dowered with blessings,
And the dog with joyous barking
Told the same, as best he could.
MARY HOWITT. *Tobias' Dog*

BUT I meäns fur to maäke 'is owd aäge as
'appy as iver I can,
Fur I owäs owd roäver moor nor I iver owäd
mottal man.
TENNYSON. *Owd Roä*

A BULLDOG of the true British breed
SIR W. SCOTT. *The Pirate*

Have a care of a silent dog.
Old Proverb

A BARK, loud, open, and free,
As an honest old watch-dog's bark should be.
Ingoldsby Legends. The Witches' Frolic.

ANIMALS are such agreeable friends; they ask
no questions, they pass no criticisms.
GEORGE ELIOT.

THE DACHSHUND   CHEPPING PUMPERNICKEL

DEAR little friend, who, day by day,
Before the door of home,
Art ready waiting till thy master come,
With monitory paw and noise.
LEWIS MORRIS.

OF all the boons that men possess,
To aid to cheer, instruct and bless;
The dog ... bold, fond and beauteous beast,
Is far from either last, or least.
ELIZA COOK.

MEGLIO é esser capo di lucertola
Che coda di dragone.
Italian Proverb

HE is the dog of one now dead; ...
His strength, his plight, his speed so light,
You had with wonder viewed.
MAGINN. *Odysseus and Argus.*

SURMOUNTING e'en her timid nature,
Love brought her to the prison door,
And there she crouched fond and faithful creature!
CAROLINE SOUTHEY. *Tale of the Reign of Terrier.*

A HEALTH to the noble, the honest old Tray,
The watchman of night, the companion of day.
ELIZA COOK.

ONE hound he had, both curious and bold,
Pleasant, but peir and full of pulchritude,
Supple and swift, and in all game richt gude.
STEWART. *Battle about a Dog.*

AN old dog cannot alter his way of barking.
Old Proverb.

BLESSINGS on thee, dog of mine.
E.B BROWNING.

"NO," said he, "I will now take a bribe to betray my
master."
Aesop's Fables.

HE must have a piece of flannel in his basket
this winter, and I shouldn't wonder if he
came out quite fresh again with the
flowers in the spring.
DICKENS. *David Copperfield.*

WHEN up they gat, and shook their lugs,
Rejoiced they were na men, but dogs!
BURNS. *Twa Dogs.*

AND a song for the dog shall be merrily
trolled,
As the meed of the faithful, the fond and the
bold.
ELIZA COOK.

"SLIPPED!"

Mrs Oliver Lucas's 'Blondie Locks' and Lieut.-Colonel Heseltine's 'Joe's Hunger' being slipped in the Sussex Oaks at the South of England Coursing Club's meeting at Woodhorne Farm, Bognor Regis, in 1937.

Photo Sport and General

HE listens for his trusty hounds.
SCOTT . The Wild Huntsman.

THE best dog leaps the stile first
Old Proverb.

ALL other houndis he did exceed sae far
As into licht the moon does near ilk star.
STEWART. *Battle about a Dog.*

LOVED Towser was his heart's delight,
Entrusted with the flocks at night,
And guardian in the field.
GALDEN. *Towser.*

OLD dogs bark not for nothing.
Proverb.

THE hounds ... divide, the loved caresses
of the mind.
SCOTT. *The Island.*

OLD dogs bark not for nothing.
Proverb.

THE hounds ... divide, the loved caresses
of the mind.
SCOTT. *The Island.*

THEY watched a cur before the miser's gate-
Gaunt, savage, shaggy, with an eye that shone...
His master prized him much.
CRABBE. *The Miser's only Friend.*

TO abandon the faithful and devoted is an endless
crime, like the murder of a Brahmin;
Never, therefore, come weal or woe, will I abandon
yon faithful dog.
Indian Hero's Creed.

TWO dogs of black St. Hubert's breed,
Unmatched for courage, breath, and speed,
Fast on his flying traces came.
SCOTT. *The Chase*

WHEN a dog has any trouble with a well-bred
biped, one may bet one's last biscuit it is
generally his own fault.
TOWNSEND. *Thoroughbred Mongrel.*

QUI veut battre son chien trouve assez de
batons.
French Proverb.

I WATCH the dog, I watch the gate.
MASSEY.

FROM many a day-dream has thy short, quick
bark
Recalled my soul.
SOUTHEY. *Death of a Favourite Dog.*

Flott Sonnenberg 668; red. Breeder, Fr. Meyer. Owner, Stuttgart Kennel Club.

SEPTEMBER

Then here we halt on the horns of a dilemma.
Everyone with large acquaintance, with
decent and "gentle-man like" dogs, must
admit their share in the highest humani-
ties;… yet shall we , because we walk
on our hind feet, assume to ourselves only
the privilege of imperishability? Shall
we, who are even as they, though we wag
our tongues and not out tails, demand a
special providence and a selfish salvation?

GEORGE ELIOT.

POOR Tray Charmant!
Poor Tray de mon ami!
Dogberry and Verges.

HUMBLE his mind, tho' great his wit.
SOMERVILLE. *All Accomplished Rover.*

WITH eye of sloe. With ear not low,
With horse's breast with depth of chest,
With breadth of loin, and curve in groin,
With nape far set behind the head:
Such were the dogs that Fingal bred.
Old Celtic Poem.

ALTHOUGH I mean not to disparage the deedes
of Alexander's horse, I will match my
dogge against him for good carriage.
SIR JOHN DAVIES in 1608.

ROUND this sepulchral spot,
Emblems of hope we twine;
If God be Love, what sleeps below was not
Without a spark divine.
Miss W. Wynn on the Death of her Dog.

OUR doggie he cam' home at e'en
And scarted both his lugs, O!
Quo he, "If folks had only tails,
They'd be maist as gude as dogs, O!
MACLEOD. *The Waggin' o' our Dog's Tail.*

THEREFORE to this dog will I,
Tenderly, not scornfully,
Render praise and favour.
E. B BROWNING. *To Flush, my Dog.*

OH! What shall I do for a dog?
HOOD. *Lament of the Blind.*

MY faithful, grateful Hector!
HOGG. *My Auld Hector.*

I WATCH the door, I watch the gate,
I'm watching early, watching late-
Your doggie still- I watch and wait!
MASSEY. *Dead Boy's Dog.*

Crooked and straight-legged Dachshund according to Buffon.

AND so my dog and I have met, and sworn
Fresh love and fealty for another morn.
RAWNSLEY. *My dog and I.*

DO the work that's nearest,
Tho' it's dull at whiles;
Helping, when you meet them,
Lame dogs over stiles.
C.KINGSLEY

HIS lungs are good enough, and his dislikes
are not at all feeble. He has a good
many years before him, no doubt.
DICKENS. *David Copperfield.*

HE would wag his three miles of a tail, and
utter soft whimperings of welcome in his
dreams.
DU MAURIER. *Trilby.*

SEE how yon terrier gently leads along
The feeble beggar to his 'customed stand.
PRATT. *Blind Man's Dog.*

THE dog and I are both grown old...
I marked his look of faithful care,
I placed my hand on his shaggy side-
"There is a sun that shines above,
A sun that shines on both," I cried.
BOWLES. *Grown Old Together.*

MY Dog! What remedy remains,
Since, teach you all I can;
I see you, after all my pains,
So much resemble man .
COWPER. *Beau and the Bird.*

THUS is there a moral obligation between a
man and a dog.
WOLCOT.

"WHAT is become of your dog, Sir John?"
"Gone to heaven," was the answer.
SOUTHEY. *Common Place Book.*

AND the dog is still the faithful,
Still the loving friend of man;
Ever ready at his bidding,
Doing for him all he can.
Sketches of Natural History.

THE drawing-room was made for dogs,
Not dogs for the drawing room.
RHODA BROUGHTON. *The Game and the Candle.*

GIVE I back more love again
Than dogs often take of men,
Learning from my human.
E.B.BROWNING. *To Flush, my Dog.*

Isolani Forst 1430; black and tan. Breeder, Förster Strecker. Owner, Count Wurmbrand.

WHATEVER sad mischance o'ertake ye,
Man, here is ane will hald ye dear!
Man, here is ane will ne'er forsake ye!
HOGG. *My Auld Hector.*

ISSA, than a maid more fond;
Issa, Indian gems beyond;
Issa, most enchanting chub!
Pup, the darling of my Pub!
ELPHINSTON. *Issa's Portrait.*

TRUE from the first, and faithful to the end,
I balk no mistress, and forsake no friend,...
A very plain and downright honest dog.
WILLIAM HAMILTON. *The Dog Incog.*

LO, the poor Indian! Whose untutor'd mind
Sees God in clouds, or hears Him in the wind;
... Thinks, admitted to that equal sky,
His faithful dog shall bear him company.
POPE. *A Simple Faith.*

THOU art as fair and comely as a dog,
Thou art as true and honest as a dog,
Thou art as kind and liberal as a dog,
Thou art as wise and valiant as a dog!
DAVIES. *In Cineam.*

AND now at last (good faith) I plainly see,
That dogs, more wise than women, friendly be.
TUBERVILLE. *Love Me, Love my Dog.*

OF any beast none is more faithful found,…
Nor keeps his master's person or his goods
With greater care than doth the dog or hound.
MOLLE. *The Faithfullest Beast.*

I NEVER barked when out of season,
I never bit without reason;
I ne'er insulted weaker brother,
Nor wronged by force or fraud another.
BLACKLOCK. *A Proud Boast.*

OF all the dogges near your father's courte,
not one hathe more love, more diligence
to please, or less paye for pleasinge, than
him I write of.
Sir J Davies to Prince Henry, 1608

BRUTE, with a heart of human love
And speechless soul of instinct fine!
How few by reason's law who more
Deserve an epitaph like thine.
FANNY KEMBLE. *On an Irish Retriever.*

Rotschild 2214; red. Breeder and owner, G. Elsässer.

OCTOBER

And this dog was satisfied
If a pale, thin hand would glide
Down his dewlaps sloping-
Which he pushed his nose within
After platforming his chin
On the palm left open…
Yet blessed to the height
Of all good, and all delight,
Previous to thy nature-
Only loved beyond that line
With a love that answers time,
Loving fellow creature.

E.B.BROWNING.
To Flush, my Dog.

BUT chief myself I will enjoin,
Awake at Duty's call;
To show a love as prompt as thine,
To him who gives me all.
COWPER. *Beau and the Water Lily.*

FOR herself she hath no fears,
Him alone she sees and hears.
WORDSWORTH. *Incident.*

AS for brute animals, and things undignified
with reason, use them generously and
nobly.
MARCUS AURELIUS.

WHAT are ye all, dear creatures tame and wild,
What other nature yours, than of a child!
LEWIS MORRIS. *To the Tormentors.*

WE hae a dog that wags his tail
(He's abit of a wag himsel', O!)
Every day he gangs down the town,
At nicht he's news to tell, O!
MACLEOD. *The Waggin' o' our Dog's Tail.*

MY dog loves me, but could he look beyond
His earthly master, would his love extend
To Him... I will not doubt.
HOLMES. *Questions.*

UNDERNEATH my stroking hand,
Startled eyes of hazel bland,
Kindling, growing larger.
E.B BROWNING. *To Flush, my Dog.*

DON and Sancho, Tranp and Tray,
On the parlour steps collected;
Wagged their tails, and seemed to say:
"Our master knows you, you're expected!"
PRAED. *Dog's Welcome.*

Komet 2365; black and tan (killed at the age of nineteen years). Breeder, H. Wiekert. Owner, H. Sprötge.

THE sleek and the gamesome, the swift and
the bold,
At surprise, I wakened to hear thy proud bark,
With the coo of the house dove, the lay of the
lark.
MOIR. *Dying Oscar.*

AY, his friend; for where shall there ever be
found
A friend like his resolute, fond, bloodhound.
BARRY CORNWALL. *My Bloodhound.*

'TIS sweet to know there is an eye will mark
Our coming, and look brighter when we come.
BRYON. *The Watch Dog.*

MY poor old Chloe! Gentle playfellow,
Most patient, most enduring was thy love.
CAROLINE SOUTHEY. *On Trust.*

MY playful cat, and honest dog,
Are all the friends I have.
ELIOT. *My Only Friends.*

SAY thou wilt course; thy greyhounds are as
swift
As breathéd stags, aye, fleeter than the roe.
SHAKESPEARE.
Taming of the Shrew. Induction, Scene 2 .

NOW let Ulysses praise his dogge Argus…
Yet could I say such things of my Bungey
as might shame them both, either for
good faith, clear wit, or wonderful deedes.
SIR JOHN DAVIES.

COME, my auld towzy, trusty friend…
All wordly cares we'll leave behind.
HOGG. *To Hector.*

DOG Rover shall confute you all;…
Can apprehend, judge, syllogise…
Is often wiser than his master.
SOMERVILLE. *All-Accomplished Rover.*

BEHOLD this creature's form and state
Which Nature therefore did create,
That to the world might be expressed
What mien there can be in a beast.
K. PHILLIPS. *The Greyhound.*

ARE clepped all by the name of dogs; the valued file
Distinguished the swift, the slow, the subtle,
The housekeeper, the hunter, everyone according
To the gift which bounteous nature hath in him
closed.
SHAKESPEARE. *Macbeth, iii. I*

HE called his dog (that sometime had the praise)
Whitefoot, well known to all that kept the plain.
DRAYTON. *Farewell to Whitefoot.*

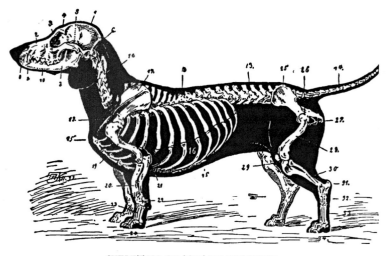

SKELETON OF THE DACHSHUND
(After the picture of the skeleton of the famous Liesel Diesch)

1, Skull. 2, Upper Jaw. 3, Eye-socket. 4, Superciliary arch. 5, Zygomatic arch. 6, Occipital bone. 7, Lower Jaw. 8, Incisors. 9, Canines. 10, Molars. 11, Cervical vertebræ (7). 12, Dorsal vertebræ (13). 13, Lumbar vertebræ. 14, Caudal vertebræ. 15, Breast-bone. 16, Chest (9 true and 4 false ribs). 17, Shoulder-blade. 18, Shoulder-joint. 19, Upper-arm (brachium). 20, Forearm (radius and ulna). 21, Elbow. 22, Wrist (carpus). 23, Metacarpal bone. 24, Toes (5 of 5 joints each). 25, Pelvic Bone. 26, Pelvic Joint. 27, Ischium. 28, Thigh. 29, Knee-joint and shin. 30, Shank. 31, Heel. 32, Tarsus. 33, Metatarsal Bone. 34, Back-toes (4 of 3 joints each).

PUT on thy envious spectacles, and see…
The dog is graced, comparèd with great Banks,
Both beasts right famous for their pretty pranks.
HARINGTON.

CALL him, he leaves his game and comes to
thee
With wagging tail, off'ring his service meek.
MOLLE. *The Faithfullest Beast.*

NOR words nor honours can enough commend
The social dog-nay , more- the faithful friend.
UNKNOWN.

IS a man a hopeless heathen if he dreams of
one fair day,
When, with spirit free from shadows grey
and cold,
He may wander thro' the heather in the
"unknown far away"
With his good old dog before him, as of old?
HORSFIELD. *Old Rocket.*

BUT all those virtues which commend...
Were thine in store, thou faithful friend,
A mate how dear!
MATTHEW ARNOLD. *Kasier Dead.*

FOR thou didst give to me, old friend,
Thy service while thy life did last.
FANNY KEMBLE. *On an Irish Retriever.*

THE fleetest, bravest hound
That ever coursed on hill or lea
... My Marmion!
MARY R. MITFORD. *Fleet Marmion.*

HOW snugly we slept in my old coat of grey,
And he licked me for kindness- my poor
dog Tray.
CAMPBELL. *Poor Dog Tray.*

HERE rest the relics of a friend below,
Blest with more sense than half the folks I
know.
PETER PINDAR
Epitaph to a Spaniel.

NOR last, forget thy faithful dogs.
DRYDEN. *The Uses of the Dog.*

TO all this fame he rose,
Only following his nose.
And, your wonder vain to shorten,
Pointer to Sir John Throckmorton.
COWPER. *A Riddle.*

ROUGH-COATED DACHSHUNDS.

NOVEMBER

*Atheism destroys magnanimity… for, take
an example of a dog, and mark what
a generosity and courage he will put on
when he finds himself maintained by a
man, who to him is instead of a God.*

BACON.

I BEGGED old Donald hard- they gave him me-
And we have lived together in this house
Long years, with no companions.
BUCHANAN. *The School Master's Story.*

HIS strength, his plight, his speed so light,
You had with wonder viewed.
MAGINN. *Argus.*

DOGS begin in jest and end in earnest.
Old Proverb.

AND as he grew older
Every beholder
Agreed he grew handsomer, sleeker and bolder.
Ingolsby Legends.

RESTING his head upon his master's knees,
Upon the bank beside him Theron lay.
What matters change of state and circumstance
to him.
ROBERT SOUTHEY. *Roderick's Faithful Theron.*

A LOVING creature she brave!
And fondly strives her struggling friend to save.
WORDSWORTH. *Dog's Tragedy.*

AND till great Snowdon's rocks grow old,
And cease the storm to brave,
The consecrated spot shall hold
The name of "Gelert's Grave!"
SPENSER. *Beth Gelert.*

THE King therefore he did give every man
Of the best houndis were amoung them.
STEWART. *Battle about a Dog.*

Photo]   *[Dorien Leigh.*

KEEPING THEM DRY.

Dogs have a great aversion to rain. The owner of these two Dachshunds, in wet weather, dresses his dogs in mackintoshes.

OF the dog in ancient story
Many a pleasant tale is told.
MARY HOWITT. *Tobias' Dog.*

THE Proverb old is verified in you;
Love me and love my dog, and so, adieu!
TURBERVILLE. *Love Me, Love my Dog.*

IN summer's heat he follows by the pace,
In winter's cold he never leaveth thee;
In mountains wild he by thee close doth trace;
In all thy fears and dangers true is he.
MOLLE. *Faithfullest Beast.*

A WITTY writer of this time
Doth make some mention in a pleasant rhyme
Of Lepidies, and of his famous dog.
HARINGTON. *In praise of Bungey.*

'TWAS set up above the lave,
The gentle hound was to me slave.
LYNDSAY. *Bagsche's Complaint.*

COME, Herod, my hound, from stranger's
floor!
Old friend, we must wander the world once
more!
BARRY CORNWALL. *My Bloodhound.*

THE dog beside the threshold lies
Mocking sleep, with half shut eyes-
Then quick he pricks his ears to hark,
And bustles up to growl and bark.
CLARKE. *The Guardian.*

THEN I was a schoolboy, all thoughtless and
free,
And thou wert a whelp, full of gambol and
glee.
MOIR. Old Oscar.

UP he sprang in eager haste,
Fawning, fondling, breathing fast
In a tender trouble.
E.B.BROWNING. *To Flush, My dog.*

THROUGH drifted snow, with ears thrown back,
I'm ready, night or day,
To follow fearless on the track
Of every beast of prey.
MARTIN. *Brave Dog's Challenge.*

I FEEL a creeping towards me-a soft head-
And on my face
A tender nose, and cold...
That is the way, you know, that dog's embrace.
RAWNSLEY. *We Meet at Morn, my Dog and I.*

I BOUGHT a dog- a queen!
Ah, Tiny dear departing pug!
She lives, but she is past sixteen.
CALVERLEY. *Disasters.*

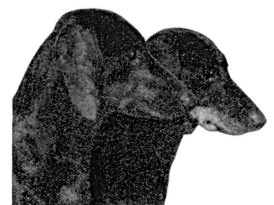

ARISTOCRATS.

Two handsome Dachshunds belonging to Mrs. Basil Huggins.

NOW beat the hound no more!
Give o'er thy cruel blows, he cried; a man's
soul verily
Is lodged in that same crouching beast.
SIR E. ARNOLD. *The Pythagorean.*

DAY after day I have come and sat
Beseechingly upon the mat,
Wistfully wondering what you are at!
MASSEY. *Dead Boy's Portrait.*

DEAR little friend, who, day by day,
Before the door of home,
Art ready waiting till thy master come.
LEWIS MORRIS. *To the Tormentors.*

WHY should not a dog have a soul like any
other respectable Christian?
Buchanan to G. Lewis.
I ONCE had a sheep-dog for guide.
HOOD. *Lament of a Poor Blind.*

AN hunde there was beside
That was yclep Hodain,
Togider thai gun abide
In joy and ek in pain.
THOMAS THE RHYMER, 1226

GO, like the Indian, in another life,
Expect thy dog, thy bottle, and thy wife,
An Essay on Man, Epis. iv.

THE dame made a curtsey,
The dog made a bow;
The dame said, "Your servant,"
The dog said, "Bow-wow."
UINKNOWN.

THE fleetest hound in all the north-
Brave Lufra saw, and darted forth.
SCOTT. *Lufra Avenged.*

THE royal hunter his brave hound caressed,
Launded his zeal and spirit unsubdued.
HOGG. *The Deep-Toned Jowler.*

FEW, at the date, arrive of ancient Argus,
Kind, sagacious brute!
Not e'en Minerva's wisdom could conceal
Thy much-loved master from thy nicer sense.
SOMERVILLE. *The chase.*

Photo]   *[E.N.A.*

FROM AUSTRIA.

There is something very intriguing about the young Dachshund, as will be seen by this photo from Vienna of a typical mother and her family.

DECEMBER

...Mine is no narrow creed;
And He how gave thee being did not frame
The mystery of life, to be the sport
Of merciless man! There is another world
For all that live and move- a better one!
Where the proud bipeds, who would fain confine
Infinite goodness to the little bounds
Of their own charity, may envy thee.

ROBERT SOUTHEY.
Canine Immortality.

AND now, with many a frisk,
Wide scampering, snatches up the drifted snow
With ivory teeth, or ploughs it with his snout,
Then shakes his powdered coat, and barks for joy.
COWPER. *The Task.*

OFT listening how the hounds and horn
Cheerily rose the slumbering morn,
From the side of some hoar hill
Through the high wood echoing shrill.
MILTON. *L'Allegro.*

I COULDN'T have any other dog but Jip; it would
be so unkind to Jip.
DICKENS. *David Copperfield.*

BLESSINGS on thee, dog of mine.
… Hands of gentle motion fail
Nevermore to pat thee!
E.B BROWNING. *To Flush, my Dog.*

NO joy did divide us; no peril could part
The man from his friend of the noble heart.
BARRY CORNWALL. *My Bloodhound.*

AN' e sarved me so well when 'e lived, that when
'e comes to be deäd,
I thinks as I'd like fur to have some soort o' a
sarvice reaä.
TENNYSON. *Owd Roä.*

THOUGH solitude around is spread,
Master, alone thou shalt not be.
BOWLES. *Grown Old Together.*

A MATE how dear.
MATTHEW ARNOLD. *Kaiser Dead.*

NOT long after Tray did the shepherd remain,
…Oh, bury me, neighbours, beside my old
friend.
PETER PINDAR. *Old Friends.*

EVEN pearls are dark before the whiteness of his
teeth.
ALGER. *Charity's Eyes.*

Photo]

WHAT CAN IT BE ?

[Fall.

Two youthful Smooth Dachshunds, the property of Mrs. Huggins, are here seen displaying an alert interest in something "off-stage"
The keen expression is very typical.

BETTER dog one wouldn't wish for in his way.
HORSFIELD. *Old Rocket.*

SELECT a few, and form them by degrees
To stricter discipline.
SOMERVILLE. *The Chase.*

THIS dog hath so himself subdued,
… And his behaviour does confess
True courage dwells with gentleness.
KATHERINE PHILLIPS. *The Trick Greyhound.*

NOW, Pilos, see how mannerly your cur,
Yon well-taught dog, that hath so many tricks.
BROWNE. *A Comedy.*

I AM misanthropos, and hate mankind.
For my part, I do wish thou wert a dog
That I might love thee.
SHAKESPEARE. *Timon of Athens, iv 3*

TO please but thee he spareth for no pains,
His hurt (for thee) is greatest good to him.
MOLLE. *The Faithfullest Beast.*

HE growled in anger, and in love caressed,
No human falsehood lurked beneath his heart;
Brave without boasting, generous without art.
UNKNOWN. *Lord Orrery's Hector.*

EHEU! Hic jacet Crony,
A dog of much renown,
Nec fur, nec macaroni,
Though born and bed in town.
UNKNOWN. *Dog Latin.*

YET hath not Jockie, nor yet Willie, seen a dog
more nimble than is this of mine.
BROWNE. *A Comedy.*

IN fields abroad he looks unto thy flocks,
Keeping them safe from wolves and other
beasts.
MOLLE. *The Faithfullest Beast.*

SIX years ago I brought him down
A baby dog, from London town;
Round his small throat of black and brown
A ribbon blue.
MATTHEW ARNOLD. *Kaiser.*

… YET here at nights I sit
Reading the Book, with Donald at my side;
I sometimes gaze in Donald's patient eyes,
So sad, so human, though he cannot speak.
BUCHANAN. *The Schoolmaster's Story.*

MOST beloved of masters, pray don't go to bed;
You had much better sit up and pat me instead!
BARHAM. *Sancho, the Bagman's Dog.*

Photo]   [Dorien Leigh.

AN INTERLUDE.

The serious business of learning seems to be endangered by the accidental meeting of a schoolboy and a Dachshund puppy
Young Dachshunds are such playful little fellows.

AND as he is thy faithful bodyguard,
So he is good within a fort or hold
Against a quick surprise to watch and ward.
MOLLE.

THE king a welp he brought
Bifor Tristrem the trewe;
… Silke was non so soft;
He was red, grene, and blewe.
THOMAS THE RHYMER, 1226

MY name came first from Holy Hubert's race,
Soygllard, my sire, a hound of singular grace.
JAQUES DU FOUILLOUX.

THE best dog in the east-nook coast.
HAMILTON. *Bonny Heck.*

THE greyhound; the great hound! The graceful
of limb!
Rough fellow! Tall fellow! Swift fellow, and
slim!
An old MS.

WE country dogs love noble sport,
And scorn the pranks of dogs at court.
UNKNOWN. *Bounce to Top.*

A VERY plain and downright honest dog.
HAMILTON. *The Dog Incog.*

IN sooth he was a peerless hound,
The gift of royal John.
SPENSER. *Beth Gelert.*

THE best of all friends.
BARRY CORNWALL. *My Bloodhound.*

I WONDER who'll have yer, my beauty,
When him as you're all to's dead.
SIMS *Told to the Missionary.*

ILKA dog has his day, O.
MACLEOD.

OBEDIENCE to a master's will
Had taught the dog to roam,
And through the terrors of the waste
To fetch the wanderer home.
CAROLINE FRY. *The Dog of St. Bernard's*

COULD well understand
The word of command,
And appear to doze
With a crust on his nose…
As he sat up on end on his little cocktail.
BARHAM. *Sancho.*

HE meant to have helped him again,
Thereto he did all his main,
Great kindness is in houndis!
Mediaval Romance, ii

IT is not from unwillingness to praise,
Or want of love, that here no stone we raise;
More thou deservest,
But *this* man gives to man,
Brother to brother, this is all we can
Get, they to whom thy virtues made thee dear
Shall find thee through all changes of the year.
WORDSWORTH.

2011

January
```
Su Mo Tu We Th Fr Sa
                   1
 2  3  4  5  6  7  8
 9 10 11 12 13 14 15
16 17 18 19 20 21 22
23 24 25 26 27 28 29
30 31
```

February
```
Su Mo Tu We Th Fr Sa
       1  2  3  4  5
 6  7  8  9 10 11 12
13 14 15 16 17 18 19
20 21 22 23 24 25 26
27 28
```

March
```
Su Mo Tu We Th Fr Sa
       1  2  3  4  5
 6  7  8  9 10 11 12
13 14 15 16 17 18 19
20 21 22 23 24 25 26
27 28 29 30 31
```

April
```
Su Mo Tu We Th Fr Sa
                1  2
 3  4  5  6  7  8  9
10 11 12 13 14 15 16
17 18 19 20 21 22 23
24 25 26 27 28 29 30
```

May
```
Su Mo Tu We Th Fr Sa
 1  2  3  4  5  6  7
 8  9 10 11 12 13 14
15 16 17 18 19 20 21
22 23 24 25 26 27 28
29 30 31
```

June
```
Su Mo Tu We Th Fr Sa
          1  2  3  4
 5  6  7  8  9 10 11
12 13 14 15 16 17 18
19 20 21 22 23 24 25
26 27 28 29 30
```

July
```
Su Mo Tu We Th Fr Sa
                1  2
 3  4  5  6  7  8  9
10 11 12 13 14 15 16
17 18 19 20 21 22 23
24 25 26 27 28 29 30
31
```

August
```
Su Mo Tu We Th Fr Sa
    1  2  3  4  5  6
 7  8  9 10 11 12 13
14 15 16 17 18 19 20
21 22 23 24 25 26 27
28 29 30 31
```

September
```
Su Mo Tu We Th Fr Sa
             1  2  3
 4  5  6  7  8  9 10
11 12 13 14 15 16 17
18 19 20 21 22 23 24
25 26 27 28 29 30
```

October
```
Su Mo Tu We Th Fr Sa
                   1
 2  3  4  5  6  7  8
 9 10 11 12 13 14 15
16 17 18 19 20 21 22
23 24 25 26 27 28 29
30 31
```

November
```
Su Mo Tu We Th Fr Sa
       1  2  3  4  5
 6  7  8  9 10 11 12
13 14 15 16 17 18 19
20 21 22 23 24 25 26
27 28 29 30
```

December
```
Su Mo Tu We Th Fr Sa
             1  2  3
 4  5  6  7  8  9 10
11 12 13 14 15 16 17
18 19 20 21 22 23 24
25 26 27 28 29 30 31
```

2012

January
```
Su Mo Tu We Th Fr Sa
 1  2  3  4  5  6  7
 8  9 10 11 12 13 14
15 16 17 18 19 20 21
22 23 24 25 26 27 28
29 30 31
```

February
```
Su Mo Tu We Th Fr Sa
          1  2  3  4
 5  6  7  8  9 10 11
12 13 14 15 16 17 18
19 20 21 22 23 24 25
26 27 28 29
```

March
```
Su Mo Tu We Th Fr Sa
                1  2  3
 4  5  6  7  8  9 10
11 12 13 14 15 16 17
18 19 20 21 22 23 24
25 26 27 28 29 30 31
```

April
```
Su Mo Tu We Th Fr Sa
 1  2  3  4  5  6  7
 8  9 10 11 12 13 14
15 16 17 18 19 20 21
22 23 24 25 26 27 28
29 30
```

May
```
Su Mo Tu We Th Fr Sa
       1  2  3  4  5
 6  7  8  9 10 11 12
13 14 15 16 17 18 19
20 21 22 23 24 25 26
27 28 29 30 31
```

June
```
Su Mo Tu We Th Fr Sa
                1  2
 3  4  5  6  7  8  9
10 11 12 13 14 15 16
17 18 19 20 21 22 23
24 25 26 27 28 29 30
```

July
```
Su Mo Tu We Th Fr Sa
 1  2  3  4  5  6  7
 8  9 10 11 12 13 14
15 16 17 18 19 20 21
22 23 24 25 26 27 28
29 30 31
```

August
```
Su Mo Tu We Th Fr Sa
          1  2  3  4
 5  6  7  8  9 10 11
12 13 14 15 16 17 18
19 20 21 22 23 24 25
26 27 28 29 30 31
```

September
```
Su Mo Tu We Th Fr Sa
                   1
 2  3  4  5  6  7  8
 9 10 11 12 13 14 15
16 17 18 19 20 21 22
23 24 25 26 27 28 29
30
```

October
```
Su Mo Tu We Th Fr Sa
    1  2  3  4  5  6
 7  8  9 10 11 12 13
14 15 16 17 18 19 20
21 22 23 24 25 26 27
28 29 30 31
```

November
```
Su Mo Tu We Th Fr Sa
             1  2  3
 4  5  6  7  8  9 10
11 12 13 14 15 16 17
18 19 20 21 22 23 24
25 26 27 28 29 30
```

December
```
Su Mo Tu We Th Fr Sa
                   1
 2  3  4  5  6  7  8
 9 10 11 12 13 14 15
16 17 18 19 20 21 22
23 24 25 26 27 28 29
30 31
```

2013

January
Su	Mo	Tu	We	Th	Fr	Sa
	1	2	3	4	5	
6	7	8	9	10	11	12
13	14	15	16	17	18	19
20	21	22	23	24	25	26
27	28	29	30	31		

February
Su	Mo	Tu	We	Th	Fr	Sa
					1	2
3	4	5	6	7	8	9
10	11	12	13	14	15	16
17	18	19	20	21	22	23
24	25	26	27	28		

March
Su	Mo	Tu	We	Th	Fr	Sa
					1	2
3	4	5	6	7	8	9
10	11	12	13	14	15	16
17	18	19	20	21	22	23
24	25	26	27	28	29	30
31						

April
Su	Mo	Tu	We	Th	Fr	Sa
	1	2	3	4	5	6
7	8	9	10	11	12	13
14	15	16	17	18	19	20
21	22	23	24	25	26	27
28	29	30				

May
Su	Mo	Tu	We	Th	Fr	Sa
			1	2	3	4
5	6	7	8	9	10	11
12	13	14	15	16	17	18
19	20	21	22	23	24	25
26	27	28	29	30	31	

June
Su	Mo	Tu	We	Th	Fr	Sa
						1
2	3	4	5	6	7	8
9	10	11	12	13	14	15
16	17	18	19	20	21	22
23	24	25	26	27	28	29
30						

July
Su	Mo	Tu	We	Th	Fr	Sa
	1	2	3	4	5	6
7	8	9	10	11	12	13
14	15	16	17	18	19	20
21	22	23	24	25	26	27
28	29	30	31			

August
Su	Mo	Tu	We	Th	Fr	Sa
				1	2	3
4	5	6	7	8	9	10
11	12	13	14	15	16	17
18	19	20	21	22	23	24
25	26	27	28	29	30	31

September
Su	Mo	Tu	We	Th	Fr	Sa
1	2	3	4	5	6	7
8	9	10	11	12	13	14
15	16	17	18	19	20	21
22	23	24	25	26	27	28
29	30					

October
Su	Mo	Tu	We	Th	Fr	Sa
	1	2	3	4	5	
6	7	8	9	10	11	12
13	14	15	16	17	18	19
20	21	22	23	24	25	26
27	28	29	30	31		

November
Su	Mo	Tu	We	Th	Fr	Sa
					1	2
3	4	5	6	7	8	9
10	11	12	13	14	15	16
17	18	19	20	21	22	23
24	25	26	27	28	29	30

December
Su	Mo	Tu	We	Th	Fr	Sa
1	2	3	4	5	6	7
8	9	10	11	12	13	14
15	16	17	18	19	20	21
22	23	24	25	26	27	28
29	30	31				

2014

January
Su	Mo	Tu	We	Th	Fr	Sa
			1	2	3	4
5	6	7	8	9	10	11
12	13	14	15	16	17	18
19	20	21	22	23	24	25
26	27	28	29	30	31	

February
Su	Mo	Tu	We	Th	Fr	Sa
						1
2	3	4	5	6	7	8
9	10	11	12	13	14	15
16	17	18	19	20	21	22
23	24	25	26	27	28	

March
Su	Mo	Tu	We	Th	Fr	Sa
						1
2	3	4	5	6	7	8
9	10	11	12	13	14	15
16	17	18	19	20	21	22
23	24	25	26	27	28	29
30	31					

April
Su	Mo	Tu	We	Th	Fr	Sa
	1	2	3	4	5	
6	7	8	9	10	11	12
13	14	15	16	17	18	19
20	21	22	23	24	25	26
27	28	29	30			

May
Su	Mo	Tu	We	Th	Fr	Sa
				1	2	3
4	5	6	7	8	9	10
11	12	13	14	15	16	17
18	19	20	21	22	23	24
25	26	27	28	29	30	31

June
Su	Mo	Tu	We	Th	Fr	Sa
1	2	3	4	5	6	7
8	9	10	11	12	13	14
15	16	17	18	19	20	21
22	23	24	25	26	27	28
29	30					

July
Su	Mo	Tu	We	Th	Fr	Sa
	1	2	3	4	5	
6	7	8	9	10	11	12
13	14	15	16	17	18	19
20	21	22	23	24	25	26
27	28	29	30	31		

August
Su	Mo	Tu	We	Th	Fr	Sa
					1	2
3	4	5	6	7	8	9
10	11	12	13	14	15	16
17	18	19	20	21	22	23
24	25	26	27	28	29	30
31						

September
Su	Mo	Tu	We	Th	Fr	Sa
	1	2	3	4	5	6
7	8	9	10	11	12	13
14	15	16	17	18	19	20
21	22	23	24	25	26	27
28	29	30				

October
Su	Mo	Tu	We	Th	Fr	Sa
			1	2	3	4
5	6	7	8	9	10	11
12	13	14	15	16	17	18
19	20	21	22	23	24	25
26	27	28	29	30	31	

November
Su	Mo	Tu	We	Th	Fr	Sa
						1
2	3	4	5	6	7	8
9	10	11	12	13	14	15
16	17	18	19	20	21	22
23	24	25	26	27	28	29
30						

December
Su	Mo	Tu	We	Th	Fr	Sa
	1	2	3	4	5	6
7	8	9	10	11	12	13
14	15	16	17	18	19	20
21	22	23	24	25	26	27
28	29	30	31			

2015

January
Su	Mo	Tu	We	Th	Fr	Sa
				1	2	3
4	5	6	7	8	9	10
11	12	13	14	15	16	17
18	19	20	21	22	23	24
25	26	27	28	29	30	31

February
Su	Mo	Tu	We	Th	Fr	Sa
1	2	3	4	5	6	7
8	9	10	11	12	13	14
15	16	17	18	19	20	21
22	23	24	25	26	27	28

March
Su	Mo	Tu	We	Th	Fr	Sa
1	2	3	4	5	6	7
8	9	10	11	12	13	14
15	16	17	18	19	20	21
22	23	24	25	26	27	28
29	30	31				

April
Su	Mo	Tu	We	Th	Fr	Sa
			1	2	3	4
5	6	7	8	9	10	11
12	13	14	15	16	17	18
19	20	21	22	23	24	25
26	27	28	29	30		

May
Su	Mo	Tu	We	Th	Fr	Sa
					1	2
3	4	5	6	7	8	9
10	11	12	13	14	15	16
17	18	19	20	21	22	23
24	25	26	27	28	29	30
31						

June
Su	Mo	Tu	We	Th	Fr	Sa
	1	2	3	4	5	6
7	8	9	10	11	12	13
14	15	16	17	18	19	20
21	22	23	24	25	26	27
28	29	30				

July
Su	Mo	Tu	We	Th	Fr	Sa
			1	2	3	4
5	6	7	8	9	10	11
12	13	14	15	16	17	18
19	20	21	22	23	24	25
26	27	28	29	30	31	

August
Su	Mo	Tu	We	Th	Fr	Sa
						1
2	3	4	5	6	7	8
9	10	11	12	13	14	15
16	17	18	19	20	21	22
23	24	25	26	27	28	29
30	31					

September
Su	Mo	Tu	We	Th	Fr	Sa
		1	2	3	4	5
6	7	8	9	10	11	12
13	14	15	16	17	18	19
20	21	22	23	24	25	26
27	28	29	30			

October
Su	Mo	Tu	We	Th	Fr	Sa
				1	2	3
4	5	6	7	8	9	10
11	12	13	14	15	16	17
18	19	20	21	22	23	24
25	26	27	28	29	30	31

November
Su	Mo	Tu	We	Th	Fr	Sa
1	2	3	4	5	6	7
8	9	10	11	12	13	14
15	16	17	18	19	20	21
22	23	24	25	26	27	28
29	30					

December
Su	Mo	Tu	We	Th	Fr	Sa
		1	2	3	4	5
6	7	8	9	10	11	12
13	14	15	16	17	18	19
20	21	22	23	24	25	26
27	28	29	30	31		

2016

January
Su	Mo	Tu	We	Th	Fr	Sa
					1	2
3	4	5	6	7	8	9
10	11	12	13	14	15	16
17	18	19	20	21	22	23
24	25	26	27	28	29	30
31						

February
Su	Mo	Tu	We	Th	Fr	Sa
	1	2	3	4	5	6
7	8	9	10	11	12	13
14	15	16	17	18	19	20
21	22	23	24	25	26	27
28	29					

March
Su	Mo	Tu	We	Th	Fr	Sa
		1	2	3	4	5
6	7	8	9	10	11	12
13	14	15	16	17	18	19
20	21	22	23	24	25	26
27	28	29	30	31		

April
Su	Mo	Tu	We	Th	Fr	Sa
					1	2
3	4	5	6	7	8	9
10	11	12	13	14	15	16
17	18	19	20	21	22	23
24	25	26	27	28	29	30

May
Su	Mo	Tu	We	Th	Fr	Sa
1	2	3	4	5	6	7
8	9	10	11	12	13	14
15	16	17	18	19	20	21
22	23	24	25	26	27	28
29	30	31				

June
Su	Mo	Tu	We	Th	Fr	Sa
			1	2	3	4
5	6	7	8	9	10	11
12	13	14	15	16	17	18
19	20	21	22	23	24	25
26	27	28	29	30		

July
Su	Mo	Tu	We	Th	Fr	Sa
					1	2
3	4	5	6	7	8	9
10	11	12	13	14	15	16
17	18	19	20	21	22	23
24	25	26	27	28	29	30
31						

August
Su	Mo	Tu	We	Th	Fr	Sa
	1	2	3	4	5	6
7	8	9	10	11	12	13
14	15	16	17	18	19	20
21	22	23	24	25	26	27
28	29	30	31			

September
Su	Mo	Tu	We	Th	Fr	Sa
				1	2	3
4	5	6	7	8	9	10
11	12	13	14	15	16	17
18	19	20	21	22	23	24
25	26	27	28	29	30	

October
Su	Mo	Tu	We	Th	Fr	Sa
						1
2	3	4	5	6	7	8
9	10	11	12	13	14	15
16	17	18	19	20	21	22
23	24	25	26	27	28	29
30	31					

November
Su	Mo	Tu	We	Th	Fr	Sa
		1	2	3	4	5
6	7	8	9	10	11	12
13	14	15	16	17	18	19
20	21	22	23	24	25	26
27	28	29	30			

December
Su	Mo	Tu	We	Th	Fr	Sa
				1	2	3
4	5	6	7	8	9	10
11	12	13	14	15	16	17
18	19	20	21	22	23	24
25	26	27	28	29	30	31

2017

January
Su	Mo	Tu	We	Th	Fr	Sa
1	2	3	4	5	6	7
8	9	10	11	12	13	14
15	16	17	18	19	20	21
22	23	24	25	26	27	28
29	30	31				

February
Su	Mo	Tu	We	Th	Fr	Sa
			1	2	3	4
5	6	7	8	9	10	11
12	13	14	15	16	17	18
19	20	21	22	23	24	25
26	27	28				

March
Su	Mo	Tu	We	Th	Fr	Sa
			1	2	3	4
5	6	7	8	9	10	11
12	13	14	15	16	17	18
19	20	21	22	23	24	25
26	27	28	29	30	31	

April
Su	Mo	Tu	We	Th	Fr	Sa
						1
2	3	4	5	6	7	8
9	10	11	12	13	14	15
16	17	18	19	20	21	22
23	24	25	26	27	28	29
30						

May
Su	Mo	Tu	We	Th	Fr	Sa
	1	2	3	4	5	6
7	8	9	10	11	12	13
14	15	16	17	18	19	20
21	22	23	24	25	26	27
28	29	30	31			

June
Su	Mo	Tu	We	Th	Fr	Sa
				1	2	3
4	5	6	7	8	9	10
11	12	13	14	15	16	17
18	19	20	21	22	23	24
25	26	27	28	29	30	

July
Su	Mo	Tu	We	Th	Fr	Sa
						1
2	3	4	5	6	7	8
9	10	11	12	13	14	15
16	17	18	19	20	21	22
23	24	25	26	27	28	29
30	31					

August
Su	Mo	Tu	We	Th	Fr	Sa
		1	2	3	4	5
6	7	8	9	10	11	12
13	14	15	16	17	18	19
20	21	22	23	24	25	26
27	28	29	30	31		

September
Su	Mo	Tu	We	Th	Fr	Sa
					1	2
3	4	5	6	7	8	9
10	11	12	13	14	15	16
17	18	19	20	21	22	23
24	25	26	27	28	29	30

October
Su	Mo	Tu	We	Th	Fr	Sa
1	2	3	4	5	6	7
8	9	10	11	12	13	14
15	16	17	18	19	20	21
22	23	24	25	26	27	28
29	30	31				

November
Su	Mo	Tu	We	Th	Fr	Sa
			1	2	3	4
5	6	7	8	9	10	11
12	13	14	15	16	17	18
19	20	21	22	23	24	25
26	27	28	29	30		

December
Su	Mo	Tu	We	Th	Fr	Sa
					1	2
3	4	5	6	7	8	9
10	11	12	13	14	15	16
17	18	19	20	21	22	23
24	25	26	27	28	29	30
31						

2018

January
Su	Mo	Tu	We	Th	Fr	Sa
	1	2	3	4	5	6
7	8	9	10	11	12	13
14	15	16	17	18	19	20
21	22	23	24	25	26	27
28	29	30	31			

February
Su	Mo	Tu	We	Th	Fr	Sa
				1	2	3
4	5	6	7	8	9	10
11	12	13	14	15	16	17
18	19	20	21	22	23	24
25	26	27	28			

March
Su	Mo	Tu	We	Th	Fr	Sa
				1	2	3
4	5	6	7	8	9	10
11	12	13	14	15	16	17
18	19	20	21	22	23	24
25	26	27	28	29	30	31

April
Su	Mo	Tu	We	Th	Fr	Sa
1	2	3	4	5	6	7
8	9	10	11	12	13	14
15	16	17	18	19	20	21
22	23	24	25	26	27	28
29	30					

May
Su	Mo	Tu	We	Th	Fr	Sa
		1	2	3	4	5
6	7	8	9	10	11	12
13	14	15	16	17	18	19
20	21	22	23	24	25	26
27	28	29	30	31		

June
Su	Mo	Tu	We	Th	Fr	Sa
					1	2
3	4	5	6	7	8	9
10	11	12	13	14	15	16
17	18	19	20	21	22	23
24	25	26	27	28	29	30

July
Su	Mo	Tu	We	Th	Fr	Sa
1	2	3	4	5	6	7
8	9	10	11	12	13	14
15	16	17	18	19	20	21
22	23	24	25	26	27	28
29	30	31				

August
Su	Mo	Tu	We	Th	Fr	Sa
			1	2	3	4
5	6	7	8	9	10	11
12	13	14	15	16	17	18
19	20	21	22	23	24	25
26	27	28	29	30	31	

September
Su	Mo	Tu	We	Th	Fr	Sa
						1
2	3	4	5	6	7	8
9	10	11	12	13	14	15
16	17	18	19	20	21	22
23	24	25	26	27	28	29
30						

October
Su	Mo	Tu	We	Th	Fr	Sa
	1	2	3	4	5	6
7	8	9	10	11	12	13
14	15	16	17	18	19	20
21	22	23	24	25	26	27
28	29	30	31			

November
Su	Mo	Tu	We	Th	Fr	Sa
				1	2	3
4	5	6	7	8	9	10
11	12	13	14	15	16	17
18	19	20	21	22	23	24
25	26	27	28	29	30	

December
Su	Mo	Tu	We	Th	Fr	Sa
						1
2	3	4	5	6	7	8
9	10	11	12	13	14	15
16	17	18	19	20	21	22
23	24	25	26	27	28	29
30	31					

2013

January
Su	Mo	Tu	We	Th	Fr	Sa
		1	2	3	4	5
6	7	8	9	10	11	12
13	14	15	16	17	18	19
20	21	22	23	24	25	26
27	28	29	30	31		

February
Su	Mo	Tu	We	Th	Fr	Sa
					1	2
3	4	5	6	7	8	9
10	11	12	13	14	15	16
17	18	19	20	21	22	23
24	25	26	27	28		

March
Su	Mo	Tu	We	Th	Fr	Sa
					1	2
3	4	5	6	7	8	9
10	11	12	13	14	15	16
17	18	19	20	21	22	23
24	25	26	27	28	29	30
31						

April
Su	Mo	Tu	We	Th	Fr	Sa
	1	2	3	4	5	6
7	8	9	10	11	12	13
14	15	16	17	18	19	20
21	22	23	24	25	26	27
28	29	30				

May
Su	Mo	Tu	We	Th	Fr	Sa
			1	2	3	4
5	6	7	8	9	10	11
12	13	14	15	16	17	18
19	20	21	22	23	24	25
26	27	28	29	30	31	

June
Su	Mo	Tu	We	Th	Fr	Sa
						1
2	3	4	5	6	7	8
9	10	11	12	13	14	15
16	17	18	19	20	21	22
23	24	25	26	27	28	29
30						

July
Su	Mo	Tu	We	Th	Fr	Sa
	1	2	3	4	5	6
7	8	9	10	11	12	13
14	15	16	17	18	19	20
21	22	23	24	25	26	27
28	29	30	31			

August
Su	Mo	Tu	We	Th	Fr	Sa
				1	2	3
4	5	6	7	8	9	10
11	12	13	14	15	16	17
18	19	20	21	22	23	24
25	26	27	28	29	30	31

September
Su	Mo	Tu	We	Th	Fr	Sa
1	2	3	4	5	6	7
8	9	10	11	12	13	14
15	16	17	18	19	20	21
22	23	24	25	26	27	28
29	30					

October
Su	Mo	Tu	We	Th	Fr	Sa
		1	2	3	4	5
6	7	8	9	10	11	12
13	14	15	16	17	18	19
20	21	22	23	24	25	26
27	28	29	30	31		

November
Su	Mo	Tu	We	Th	Fr	Sa
					1	2
3	4	5	6	7	8	9
10	11	12	13	14	15	16
17	18	19	20	21	22	23
24	25	26	27	28	29	30

December
Su	Mo	Tu	We	Th	Fr	Sa
1	2	3	4	5	6	7
8	9	10	11	12	13	14
15	16	17	18	19	20	21
22	23	24	25	26	27	28
29	30	31				

2014

January
Su	Mo	Tu	We	Th	Fr	Sa
			1	2	3	4
5	6	7	8	9	10	11
12	13	14	15	16	17	18
19	20	21	22	23	24	25
26	27	28	29	30	31	

February
Su	Mo	Tu	We	Th	Fr	Sa
						1
2	3	4	5	6	7	8
9	10	11	12	13	14	15
16	17	18	19	20	21	22
23	24	25	26	27	28	

March
Su	Mo	Tu	We	Th	Fr	Sa
						1
2	3	4	5	6	7	8
9	10	11	12	13	14	15
16	17	18	19	20	21	22
23	24	25	26	27	28	29
30	31					

April
Su	Mo	Tu	We	Th	Fr	Sa
		1	2	3	4	5
6	7	8	9	10	11	12
13	14	15	16	17	18	19
20	21	22	23	24	25	26
27	28	29	30			

May
Su	Mo	Tu	We	Th	Fr	Sa
				1	2	3
4	5	6	7	8	9	10
11	12	13	14	15	16	17
18	19	20	21	22	23	24
25	26	27	28	29	30	31

June
Su	Mo	Tu	We	Th	Fr	Sa
1	2	3	4	5	6	7
8	9	10	11	12	13	14
15	16	17	18	19	20	21
22	23	24	25	26	27	28
29	30					

July
Su	Mo	Tu	We	Th	Fr	Sa
		1	2	3	4	5
6	7	8	9	10	11	12
13	14	15	16	17	18	19
20	21	22	23	24	25	26
27	28	29	30	31		

August
Su	Mo	Tu	We	Th	Fr	Sa
					1	2
3	4	5	6	7	8	9
10	11	12	13	14	15	16
17	18	19	20	21	22	23
24	25	26	27	28	29	30
31						

September
Su	Mo	Tu	We	Th	Fr	Sa
	1	2	3	4	5	6
7	8	9	10	11	12	13
14	15	16	17	18	19	20
21	22	23	24	25	26	27
28	29	30				

October
Su	Mo	Tu	We	Th	Fr	Sa
			1	2	3	4
5	6	7	8	9	10	11
12	13	14	15	16	17	18
19	20	21	22	23	24	25
26	27	28	29	30	31	

November
Su	Mo	Tu	We	Th	Fr	Sa
						1
2	3	4	5	6	7	8
9	10	11	12	13	14	15
16	17	18	19	20	21	22
23	24	25	26	27	28	29
30						

December
Su	Mo	Tu	We	Th	Fr	Sa
	1	2	3	4	5	6
7	8	9	10	11	12	13
14	15	16	17	18	19	20
21	22	23	24	25	26	27
28	29	30	31			

Material in this diary has been sourced from the following titles:

J. H. Walsh. *The Dogs Of The British Islands.* 1867
Vero Shaw. *The Illustrated Book Of The Dog.* 1879
Rawdon B. Lee. *A History And Description Of The Modern Dogs.* 1894
H. W. Huntington. *My Dog And I.* 1897
H. W. Huntington. *The Show Dog.* 1901
W, D. Drury. *British Dogs - Their Points, Selection, And Show Preparation.* 1903
Frank Townend Barton. *Sporting Dogs - Their Points: And Management.* 1905
James Watson. *The Dog Book - A Popular History Of The Dog.* 1906
Robert Leighton. *The New Book Of The Dog.* 1907
J. Sidney Turner. *The Kennel Encyclopaedia.* 1907
Edward C. Ash. *Dogs And How To Know Them.* 1925
Frank Townend Barton. *Hounds.* 1913
A. Croxton Smith. *About Our Dogs - The Breeds And Their Management.* 1931
Arthur Craven. *Dogs Of The World.* 1931
Walter Hutchinson. *Hutchinson's Dog Encyclopaedia.* 1935
Stanley West. *The Book Of Dogs.* 1935
Herbert C. Sanborn. *The Dachshund or Teckel.* 1937
Various. *The Dachshund - A Complete Anthology Of The Dog.* 2010

Lightning Source UK Ltd.
Milton Keynes UK
UKOW04n0625061213

222504UK00004B/11/P